Nebraska
This Place, These People

Wm. Kloefkorn

Nebraska
This Place, These People

Poems by
William Kloefkorn
State Poet of Nebraska

NEBRASKA LIFE PUBLISHING

Kloefkorn, William
Nebraska: This Place, These People/William Kloefkorn

ISBN: 978-0-9789364-9-5
Manufactured in the United States of America
First Edition/First Printing November 2010

Published by

Nebraska Life Publishing
206 West Norfolk Avenue
PO Box 819
Norfolk, NE 68702-0819
USA

Publisher/President: Christopher Amundson
Vice President: Angela Amundson

Book design by Anthony Kuhlmann
Cover and book illustrations by Anthony Kuhlmann
Back cover painting by Carlos Frey

**To buy books in quantity for corporate use or incentives,
call (800) 777-6159 or email premiums@NebraskaLife.com**

Visit us online at www.NebraskaLife.com

*This collection is respectfully dedicated
to the places and people
inside its poems,*

*wherever and whoever we are, and were,
or might yet one day
become.*

Table of Contents

Part I
Holding Forth Promise

"The land belongs to the future . . .; that's the way it seems to me. How many of the names on the county clerk's plat will be there in fifty years? I might as well try to will the sunset over to my brother's children. We come and go, but the land is always here. And the people who love it and understand it are the people who own it—for a little while."

– Alexandra, in Willa Cather's *O Pioneers!*

Cottonwood

Teach us of roots,
Of the soft diurnal showering of seed.
Aware of soil and water, speak then to us of fire:
How driftwood moves on borrowed streams,
How elemental are the gatherings.
With branches splayed
Describe the broad blue seasons,
And their winds. Say it:
Because of me the roosted bird is tiny,
The lightning more than likely.
However then transected,
Chant with your breadth a liturgy of growth rings.
Ooze from your impacted pores
The simple juice of need:
Of roots, becoming as they are,
Of the soft diurnal showering of seed.

THE EXQUISITE BEAUTY
OF SOUTHEASTERN NEBRASKA

for Cliff Fawl

It is there like a postcard, he says,
And means it.
Space for grain and apples, right enough.
And for breathing.
Calls it something gaudy,
And don't care:
The exquisite beauty, say, of southeastern Nebraska.
Grins when he says it, too, like a gopher.
Speaks then of the smell of soil
Just last night rained on.
Is there gold in these here hills?
Ask the winesaps at Nebraska City.
The milo. The corncribs south of Bennett,
dear as inlays.
(Did you know that kernels of hybrid seed
Are angels' eyeballs?)
Or question the shoreline of the Platte.
Do it however it pleases you,
But do it.
Touch it all, he says,
Even the lowdown price of hogs.
Let it run through your eyes
Like silt through fingers.
Then say something,
And mean it.
It is there like a postcard, for example,
This exquisite beauty of southeastern Nebraska.

Enough almost by god to make a fellow
Not ashamed to worship.

What the Land Says

*Land is immortal, for it harbors the mysteries
of creation.*
                    –Anwar al-Sadat, *In Search of Identity*

Though I am beneath you
I am neither docile nor subservient.
One story has it that I am

the mother of the gods, their father
the sky that having arisen
abides no end. Believe this much:

I am earth, your mother.
And believe that to nurture is to give
birth to nourishment.

Witness the cornstalk, the treeline,
the waterway. Inhale
the lilac, the new-cut clover, those

tubers so recently dug
from my body so dark and fecund.
Taste those many

children I bequeath you—blueberry,
raspberry, chokecherry,
plum. Touch with the tips of your

fingers the tips of all
things touchable—grassblade and leaf,
tassel and beak, beard

and bud—and the face of the one about
to be lowered to enhance
me, and the face of that other

looking on.

What the Sky Says

That saints will aid if men will call:
For the blue sky bends over all!
　　　　　　　–Samuel Taylor Coleridge, "Christabel"

Though I am above you
I am not beyond your fear, your eventual
human understanding.

One story has it that I am the father
of the gods,
your mother this good receptive earth

beneath me.
Believe this much: We were deeply,
desperately in love. From our immortal

offspring you and your
eternal offspring bloomed and flourished,
bloom and flourish yet,

in spite of those elements that, unduly
loosened, threaten: fire
and ice, flood and wind, eruptions from the

pit of the one that feeds
you. Believe this much: I am vastness
that in time of feast and

famine you look up to to know that you are
never alone—moonset and
starshine and cloudburst, sunglow and bird-

wing—and that child in its swing
looking to rise high as heaven on the crest
of an inland sea.

Alone in the Sandhills of Sheridan County, Nebraska, Standing Near the Grave of Mari Sandoz

She holds to her silence
as if death can be in fact
conclusive,
the lark meanwhile
from atop its perch of soapweed
stirring the warm June air
with the wand of its
high sudden song.

And this hillside, this delicate hogback,
how the late afternoon sun
shimmers its coarse green skin,
switchgrass and snakegrass and grama,
and above it all the wide bellies
of the Hereford and the Angus,
their calves beside them
red and black in the sunlight,
shimmering. And nearby the orchard,
Old Jules' apple and peach and plum trees
in a long thick line of open defiance,
beyond them the lowland meadow
sweet with impending hay,
and standing here
alone in the Sandhills
of Sheridan County, Nebraska,
near the grave of Mari Sandoz,
I would think of something true
to match the perfect pitch of the lark,
against one of the barbs guarding the grave
would puncture myself to blood
to know and to keep it:
that I am here, alive
at this X my bootheel marks
in the earth of Sheridan County,

that above me the flash of the redwing
omens the blue sky now and tomorrow,
that I am as surely the object
of the kingbird's eye as I am observer.

Until the gathering cirrus
begins to deplete the sun:
the throat of the pulley
when I push back the gravegate
whines. At my ankles
persist the burrs of lost uprisings,
lost intentions, lost loves,
while underfoot the grit
for all its eternal shifting
never moves.

Waiting for the Bus at 63rd and Huntington

No wind this morning,
not so much as the slightest move
from a single leaf on the cottonwood.
The rain clouds, after a slow heavy night,
seem spent, seem satisfied now
describing the blue of scattered sky
beyond them.

And waiting for the bus at this corner
at 63rd and Huntington
I cannot inhale deeply enough
to both catch it and keep it: your body
so fresh, so revived from its shower,
ankle and thigh, belly, nipple, lip, lash,
and the brief gracious scent
from the white flower drenched
on the linden.

AFTER THE ICE STORM

After the ice storm
I walk the campus to witness
the remarkably beautiful devastation,
ice into snow into heaviness
not even the limbs on the largest oak
could bear.

After the ice storm
I select a fallen limb from that
largest oak.
I would have it as something more
than a remnant, a token
reminder.

After the ice storm
I walk the campus with a walking-stick
smooth and as stout
as a farm boy's forearm. And I am not
surprised: it takes me back
to where it came from.

After the ice storm
I sense that time, having passed, goes right on
passing. So many survivors so
green now, so eager
to fill those many gaps
left by those who are gone.

TREMOLO

After I showed my mother my first scalp,
I stayed with the women awhile and they were
all singing and making the tremolo.
  –Black Elk in John Neihardt's *Black Elk Speaks*

Wind in the trees is the birdsong wavering,

sing center, sing circle, sing

blanket spread wide for its un-
daunted people,

sing offering, sing prayer, sing

bodies spread wide and deep
on the hillsides,

sing spirit, sing blossom, sing

ghosts on the wings of horses
now silent as stones,

sing famine, sing feast, sing

dreams in the blood and breast
of the living,

sing grass, sing bison, sing

bones.

River

I have no word for the river living inside me.
　　　　　–Denise Low, "Learning the Language of Rivers"

Because I cannot name it—this river living
inside me—

I can only respond to its movements, and
because

they are both incessant and eternal what
must I

conclude? That I too am incessant and
eternal,

that at night no less than in daylight it
bends to

bend again to wherever the everlasting
leads it, and

in my dreams the serpent that is its lean
configuration

would pose the question to which the
answer

is this: Water. The body is mostly water.

Bur Oak

This little nature book, *Bur Oak*, is yet another
I must hide from the children.

They must not hear, not yet, such sweet seductions—
catkin, bud, pollen, stalk, acorn.

All in good time. In the fall, sap runs more slowly
through the tree. Go to sleep, my children.

Go to sleep. Meanwhile, beyond the window a squirrel
lifts in its delicate paws an acorn.

In the Spring, the earth will warm again
and the tree awaken. Children,

can you hear me? I am reading you awake: a tiny root
breaks through the tip of a fallen acorn.

Can you hear it? The root burrows into the ground.
A stem appears, with bud and leaves. Children,

this baby oak will grow taller and wider every year,
given sufficient rain and sun. Once hidden, the acorn

over many moons becomes the oak you'll climb too high
in spite of all my admonitions O my children!

Nebraska, Early March

The sun one hour from setting
distinguishes the landscape,
so red the barn,
so white the house,
each weathered board
so cleanly defined
on the slatted grainbin.
And the hay, each mound,
and the cattle, each calf
beside each cow so singular
against a slope of golden stubble,
and the stubble, each stalk,
and along the roadside the bluestem, each stem, and the fenceline,
each barb, and later the moon
through the window
washing our bodies, each
member, and your hair,
under my wildest touch each
indivisible strand.

Midland's Profile

Around four o'clock the sun catches the country's best
side.

Beneath the hair of fresh stubble
a podded land puffs
high brown cheeks
toward December.
The flesh of the soil is vast and cool,
bulged, wound like a gift with wire
whose barbs burst
against a low sun's light.

Slatted grain bins go golden at the cracks.

A red deep-bedded truck sits near a barn,
half buckled under the unloaded pleasure of baled hay.

Two pheasants shuffle husks among the spilled
kernels of dinner.

Towns jut suddenly forward,
their elevators warm jowled with grain.

Wahoo. Swedeburg. Wisner. Scribner. Laurel,
all sending shards of shadow
to a late complected eastern landscape.

> The eye must count
> so fine a maze: each rich pock
> somehow photographed.
> Even the fallen seeds lie filled
> upon the portly face, genetic giants
> waiting like cattle to be fed.

And at the throat of scattered homes
the trunks of windbreakers: Pine. Cottonwood. Elm.
The switch of tamarack.
All a part of the profile,
all full lipped and facing north.

Fat, now, and quietly proud.

Pioneer Courtship

During a Saturday night dance
At the Doyle Schoolhouse,
Not far from Exeter, Nebraska,

Joe Gephardt looked up
From the spit-shine on his shoes
Into the eyes of Miss Jenny Satterfield.

Well now, he said,
And Jenny, who had spent much of the evening
Picking at her hanky,

Agreed.

Surprise Lilies

for Ted Kooser

The blind, my friend writes, always come
    as such a surprise. And so too
        these lilies,

appearing suddenly on the last dog-day
    of summer, their stems
        delicate

and as slender as the legs of that
    translucent girl in the
        seventh grade,

their petals a color I can't come up with,
    lavender, my wife tells me,
        or maybe orchid.

I prefer both—lavender into orchid—lavender
    for the sound of three
        syllables,

orchid for my grandmother's laughter
    each time she stumbled
        saying it. So

I sit on the front porch at high noon
    studying the lilies, their
        frail effrontery,

their silence, so far-flung and absolute.
    Tonight not even a full moon
        will be sufficient

for me to see them. With a length of sumac
    I'll tap my way to where
        I'll hope to find

them, until—surprise!—the solitary leaf,
    the howl, the sudden
        snow.

Walking the Campus

Under a full summer moon the hackberry
rises beyond itself, each leaf a hand
flat against a dense conglomeration
of Nebraska stars.

Old Main stands steady as a good heart's beat,
its red brick stout with ivy,
its doors beckoning
to each of the four immense directions.

I am walking the campus,
studying the books of bur oak and of pine,
around me the sticks and the cornerstones
of ages. Far down the woodchip path, the path

keeps going. Remember the face beside you
during all those eons in chemistry?
Fire is what you felt when something
turned your eyes to meet that other

eye. Now water cools the mind,
furrows the earth
from which emerge the blossom and the stem
to sanctify the air. Always

there is a country to be away from, always
just beyond the outstretched arm
a lesson ripe to be learned, always
a bed of olive or of wheatstraw to return to.

Beside a young persimmon I pause
to inhale the evening.
A woman holding the hand of a small boy
comes up the path. She is talking quietly,

explaining everything, each word distinct,
each syllable a piling up of proof that
life should be the act of paying close
attention. When I say *hello* the boy

giggles. I am at the very edge:
one more gift and I'll break
like a gathering of giddy friends
into a thousand songs.

MOSAICS

in commemoration of the Nebraska State Capitol
after fifty years, 1932-1982

Symmetry of stone and of marble,
order solid for the moment
against all threats of chaos,
you are the grand mosaic
saying how sweet it is
to have all other gods
within, a part, of you.

    I see the walking plow
    that broke the earth
    you sprouted from.
    I see the steam
    from the nostrils
    of the horses
    that pulled the plow,
    small mosaic of fetlock
    and of haunches
    in awful tandem.

Call it a seed
that gave birth to the seed
that birthed you. So
tell us, Grandmother, Father,
where does the good earth end
and the dream begin?

    Seed dropped into the furrow
    behind the walking plow
    you take root, you rise
    mightily, you grumble,
    you want to be yourself
    yet more than yourself,
    and you are, you are,
    mural, sower, tower,
    ivory, inlay, scroll,
    watchful citizen long dead
    alive in bronze,
    name deep to the touch
    in the heft of square and of circle.

I enter you
to become a part of the seed
that birthed you.
We are indeed mosaics, are we not,
all of us, the quick and the static,
palettes forever distinct with colors
and the colors flowing.

On a clear calm night
I too take root, I too rise,
I too want to be myself
yet more than myself.

    I stop somewhere
    just short of the stars,
    life at the edge of this massive calm
    upright, too clear-headed
    ever to lose. Around me, in each
    of the four great directions,
    the lights of an inland city move
    and do not move.
    Beneath my feet
    mosaic after grand mosaic
    trembles. I too tremble—
    thunderbird, buffalo, coyote, fox,
    mosaic of blood evolved
    to know what I know:

nothing solid at last
but the seed,
nothing at last more generous
than the letting go.

Platte Valley Windmill

Punch a thumb into this Platte Valley soil
and if the thumb is longer than a moment
you'll strike a mother lode
far richer even
than a good rainwater cistern.

Even so, Anna with a length of willow
witches for water. Voodoo Anna,
her wild hair stilled for the moment
beneath a scarf of red bandana,
the limb in her hands as if a plowbeam
hitched to the tough slow movement
of an invisible mare.

When the willow quivers and trembles,
and plunges downward,
Anna shouts *Hoka-hey!*
as if her own sweet skin,
and not the earth's beneath her,
had been broken.

The windmill rises straight and clean
and incredibly new,
its wheel impatient to catch the wind,
its shaft the latest onset
of perpetual motion.

The first of the water
gurgles out of the spout
and down the trough
and splashing against our hands
falls into the deep round silver metal tank.

Anna stands to shake her wet palms above me,
a little christening,
and I look up to see
a circle of sunspots
flashing their semaphore
to the remotest byway in the valley.
Whoever is thirsty, whatever is thirsty,
wherever you are, old man, old beast,
old woman, old bird,
if you are thirsty,
come, come to the well and drink.

WET SPELL

The back of the drought is broken, we say,
but there is more bile than laughter
aslosh in the belly.

We first must count the drops of water
as they scour the shingles.
Must watch the dust thicken to mud,
the color of the soil darken.
Must feel the nerves in our necks go pinched
as we watch the clouds,
expecting them at any second to disperse,
to uncover the huge consuming face
of the sun.

We push open the screendoor
and walk out, all of us children,
into the salt-sweet sting of our disbelief.
Yes, Mother, this is indeed rain,
the aftermath of which we long ago were dwarfed by
as, like Ruth, we stood transfixed
among the towering and alien corn.
It just might be possible, after all, to live again.
Do you suppose?

And the minutes pass, and the days,
and the moisture, more genuine than grief,
swells the ground. With it,
we become cisterns, filling slowly:
ankle to knee to thigh
to breast to throat,
and thoroughly slaked
we speak of the sun
as if recalling the most laughable of breeds:
a mongrel bitch with her back broken,
ho ho ho ho ho,
her tail, as if a truce,
between her legs.

Lake Leba, Early Spring

1

Rum in the veins of the cottonwood,
and a hundred thousand leaves
begin their flickering.

Above a blue flatbed of water,
cool as the underbelly of a stone,
crappie are jumping,
flexing themselves like paid performers
against a sudden burst of yellow sun.

2

Out of the small wet tombs of our dreams
we have come alive,
and along a stretch of granulated beach
we gather now,
our backs and thighs and bellies
taking in the offspring
of a generous sun.

A south wind rises.

The water begins to swell and crest
and spill itself
again, and then again,
along the sand.

We move into the nearest current,
skin and sun, wind and sand and water
becoming one.

The word in the throat of the meadowlark
is precise and clear:
O nothing short of death,
sweet death, sweet death,
can keep us from reviving here!

3

Suddenly it is so calm
we can hear the quiet crashing
of an orange sun
gone down.
We breathe out.
We breathe in.
The western star, on schedule,
explodes its film.

And the water begins to settle:
a vast and tireless mother,
it rocks the moon.

4

Wine in the bloodstream of the campfire,
and the sticks and stones of ages
let go their passion.

We raise our glasses
to touch each other's rims.
Shadows on a soft, shifting screen
project the sound

as, from across the water,
other human voices reach us,
and once again, once yet again,
in mutual awe and love,
we drown.

SCHWINN

for John Dietrich

My young son carries the fruitjar of coins
into the shop,
lifts it heavy as a sashweight
into the hands of Dietrich,
that old crippled German
who knows more about bicycles
than Carter knows about pills.

Dietrich removes the lid,
spills the coins like a miniature mountain
on the counter. What we don't tell him
is that we know to the penny
how much money the fruitjar contains:
enough money to the penny to buy that
black and white Schwinn in the window.

A line forms behind us:
a young man with twisted handlebars,
a woman with a black tube around her neck
like a blowout necklace.
But Dietrich, his glasses low
on the bridge of his nose,
keeps his attention on the coins—

not from any sense of greed,
but because he takes his customers
one at a time, youngsters especially,
each step performed both
thoroughly and to perfection.
He reminds me of my German grandmother,
including the accent. Meanwhile, he

limps to the window,
takes down the bike,
presses each tire, nods, smiles,
and I think how this is the bike
I lay awake to pray for

when I was throwing the *Beacon*,
each paperbag filled to overflowing

with Goebbels and Goering and Hitler
and Tojo and Mussolini,
this is the bike that in some
inexplicable fashion
might have hastened the victory,
might have reduced somehow the pain.

Later, on the sidewalk at home,
my son will stand tall
to reach the pedals,
and I'll give him a shove
to send him handlebars and all
sparkling on a run that will come
full circle, but not quite end.

Old Dietrich seems satisfied
that the bike is ready. Perhaps
he came directly
from the old country, too,
where my grandmother lived, his hands
large like hers delivering the bike
as if the prodigy he'd stake his life on
into the hands of my suddenly older son.

MIRACLE

. . . the song she hums is this miracle singing
inside me.
                –Laura Tohe, "The Platte"

And this miracle, she said, shall be named Moonshell,
after Moonshell River, an early name
for the Platte, and a beautiful name, she said, and how

unfortunate it is, she said, that the name was changed.
But that's the way it is with both man
and river, isn't it?—that sorry business of inflicting change

no less than standing by to receive it—so in our own
ingenuous ways we move like
braided water to contend with its snags and sawyers,

naming the miracle inside us Moonshell, such a lovely
name for whatever miracle
awaits its birth inside us, Moonshell alive and singing

in a river whose source was the first source, Moonshell
River in spite of its demise
giggling like the child it is until spent it runs into the sea.

Part II

Drifting Along:
Mother Nature Delivers

"For I am a part of the Prairie,
   Kin to the Wind and the Lightning . . .
I feel the despair of the Storm,
Rejoice with the joy of the River.
Even as these would sing in their differing
moods, I sing!"

– from the Prelude to John Neihardt's
   A Bundle of Myrrh

BOUNDARIES

At the height of winter
the current in the Platte
beneath an overhead of ice
moves on, Missouri and Mississippi
on its cold narrow mind.

In early summer I bring my boot down
hard against the ground:
the current swallows at a sudden gulp
a brick of shoreline.

So where is the piling deep enough
to fix possession,
the curbing tight enough
to keep that critter out, this critter in?

All week I rearrange the fence
along the river,
on Sunday doze to hear it one more time:
when the eye of the flesh goes shut,
O pioneer,
the eye of the spirit opens.

December Storm, Nebraska

It is here again, friends,
because again we failed
to keep the faith.

Someone somewhere lost his nerve,
went to sleep and unclenched his fists,
dropped the lower jawbone of his guard,
and this bleak new season,
big-eyed with opportunity,
ungentle in its bones,
moved in.

Even so,
it is never so warm
as when the sun's first slant
redeems the blast of evening.

We touch,
and the breaking of yet another faith
begins again.

Some Directions for the December Touring of Westcentral Nebraska

Turn right at the Standard station
And head due west. Do not
Eat at the Hungry Indian
In Ogallala or stop for

Free tea at the Big Farmer
In Oshkosh—By Gosh. My
Advice, Sir: go cold and
Hungry over these wintered ranges

Where only on a cloudless night
Can the sky outstrip the land.
Join the tumbleweed. Huddle
With Herefords against leeward

Walls. Walk barefoot over
Steaming dung along the
Dormant seeded rows of
Next year's yield. Forget

The motels at North Platte.
Tune out all noisy teepees:
KODY, KOLT, KCOW. Hum
The notes of rusting cultivators

And watch with the hawk
For mice and rabbits and
Scott's once-in-a-lifetime bluff.
Inhale. Go dizzy with the

Windmill. Stretch even the
Fingertips against sand-coated hills.
You can get there from here,
Sir. But you must go

Cold and hungry. The route is best.
Just forget your Pontiac, then
Turn right at the Standard station
And drive due west.

REFLECTION

I do not know
that the bird is not pestered
with thought.
I am not sure whether,
when the sap starts downward,
the green leaf shudders.
I wonder
about the weight of the dues
the free wind pays.
The cow that chews the damp grass
in the pasture:
at what expense
the puffing of her udder?

There is so much not to learn,
so many sprouts to leave untouched,
to let grow.
Enough to say that the bird moves
and makes its sound and is gone,
that the green leaf browns,
that the wind, like the weather,
comes and goes,
that milk is of itself
a gathering of bones.

Let us walk then without shoes
over the old earth.
Let us feel how at each falling step
we take root,
how at the lifting of each foot
we become more delicate than air.
Let us breathe in, to live by,
that which we cannot answer.

Middle Loup

Each early summer
The belly of the Middle Loup
Entertains a new life,
Collects from trees and floods of trash
Fresh spring sperm
For the crop of green June boys
Who bring their boats like wide Egyptian women
To the fertile shores of a Nebraska Nile.

On sunny afternoons,
Under a high sky,
Drifting,
The will goes soft,
Like potatoes too long in the basement,
And the boys, naked with the current,
Jab fat thumbs into the flesh of their
Thick clean unassuming playmate,
Their eyes swimming like perfect fools
Downstream,
Down anywhere,
Peeling away the
Tranquil rooted leeward bay of land:
A field of corn, a barn, a robin's nest,
A wild red flower about to bloom
Rising from the back seat
Of a disembodied Ford.

All land-locked, attached:
Deep and neat and dry as ruts
And laughable as mothers
After the cord is cut.

FRANK FAIRCHILD:
YOUNG AND A BACHELOR AND A FARMER

I'm off my feed again,
feeling lower than a bucket
in an empty cistern.
This farm I swear is shrinking faster
than a two-dollar shirt.
Nothing here anymore to milk
but the cats,
no flank bigger than a baby bruise
to lean a forehead into.

Velma Jean writes
she'll not be seeing me this summer,
she's finally landed a steady job,
with decent pay,
even if it is in Omaha,
but we can always be good friends,
can't we, Frank,
and Frank Fairchild you're certainly a
gingerheart
if there ever was one.

You ever notice how when it gets dry
it gets dry all over?
Jesus, what I'd give
for a good toad-strangling storm!
Tell you what:
if I could muster up
so much as a small single dollop of spit
I'd play the saint just long enough
to share it with the corn.

NEBRASKA HIGHWAY 83

to be sung to the tune of your choice

I'm on a long black roller-coaster,
Nebraska Highway 83.
I'm on a Sandhills roller-coaster,
just I, myself, and me.

We're driving north to Valentine.
That's where the heart is, so I'm told.
And someone in Valentine will greet me, maybe,
maybe someone with a heart of solid gold. O . . .

I'm on a long black roller-coaster,
beneath a high wide Nebraska sky.
I'm on a Sandhills roller-coaster,
just me, myself, and I.

> The Nebraska Sandhills. Eighteen thousand square miles
> of vegetated sand dunes, the largest expanse of its type
> in the western hemisphere. It's a wide-open secret under
> which lies one of the world's most spacious aquifers. Call
> it *O*. Call it *gal*. Call it *la la*. Call it *O-gal-la-la*. O . . .

I'm on a long black roller-coaster,
Nebraska Highway 83.
I'm on a Sandhills roller-coaster,
just I, myself, and me.

And that's a trio, a triad, a trinity.
That's a threesome, a triple-play.
Trio. Triad. Trinity.
Just I, myself, and me.

> That bovine over yonder is a black Angus, a black baldy,
> because of its all-white head. And you see that large hole
> in the side of that sand dune to the right? That's what they
> call a blowout. It owes its existence to a south wind that
> blew so hard that a chicken, or so they say, laid the same egg
> three times.

And that's the truth, they say,
and that's a fact, they say,
and they call it verity.
And that's a trio, a threesome, a triple-play,
a triad, a trinity. O . . .

I'm on a long black roller-coaster,
Nebraska Highway 83.
I'm on a Sandhills roller-coaster,
Just I, myself, and me.

> The Nebraska Sandhills. Eighteen thousand square miles
> of vegetated sand dunes, the largest expanse of its type
> in the western hemisphere. It's a wide-open inland sea,
> big and little bluestem moving like golden billows
> in the breeze.

I'm heading north to Valentine.
That's where the heart is, so I'm told.
And someone in Valentine will greet me, maybe,
maybe someone with a heart of solid gold. O . . .

I'm on a long black roller-coaster,
beneath a sky-blue Nebraska sky.
I'm on a Sandhills roller-coaster,
must me, myself and I.

> Sand dunes. Angus. Bluestem.
> Blowout. Inland sea.
> I'm parting the water with the bow of my boat,
> just I, myself, and me. O . . .

I'm on a long black roller-coaster,
beneath a friendly Nebraska sky.
I'm on a Sandhills roller-coaster,
just me, myself, and I.

I'm on a Sandhills roller-coaster,
just me, myself, and I.
Just me, myself, and I . . . .

Behind the Movie House, Early July

for Willa Cather

Behind the movie house, early July,
I smoke drip-grind Folgers
rolled in toilet paper,
beside me my new friend Norman
chewing eleven sticks of Yucatan,
wondering out of the vacant half of his mouth
which of the two rocks
fired earlier in the day from our slingshots
killed the lark.

At our backs, into our backs,
backs tanned and bare,
croons the voice of Gene Autry,
rhythm guitar the easy clipclop
of his horse's hooves.
When we returned at dusk
to look again at the body
it was gone. Norman said,
Cats.

On such a night, no wind,
you can smell the harvest
spilling from the dumptrucks
droning main street
from the wheatfields south of town.
A shot rings out.
Mr. Autry stops his singing.
Yellow. The belly of the lark was yellow,
defined by the blood-red blood
already clotting among the feathers
where the rock went in.

Norman chews and chews
that wad of pink-to-purple gum.
Ricochet. The word is a long song
whining to silence
beyond the boulders
that more striking even
than the golden yucca
bloom. Outlaw. One by one,
this hand abruptly
to the belly of that blood-soaked denim,

they fall
to lie face-down amazingly silent in the sand.
How do I know all this?
Norman tells me, who has seen this movie,
he says, seventy times
seven.

Years later I'll discover
that the lark has only five notes
it can sing. So shit on the pumphandle, Smiley,
what does it do?
Well shit on your own pumphandle, Gene,
it sings them.

Autry. Outlaw. Ricochet. Norman's mouth
a bolus of Yucatan, pink-to-purple gum.
The sweet smell of harvest,
the taste of coffee that never quite ignites
bitter against the tongue.

And the dream that turns to memory,
giving us, we say, that O so crucial edge,
thus making us, we say, somehow human:
small rock fired from a slingshot,
in small-town motion describing
yesterday and today and forever
the warm relentless arc
that beyond all earthly understanding
passes on.

Pissing Into the Republican

I do it
because the river is handy,
because it runs squarely through
the middle of Morrison Park,

where my brother, who beside me
likewise is doing it
into the Republican,
has driven me

to look at and to walk over
a long riverside acreage
of native prairie grasses,
all of them dormant now,

Spring yet another month away,
but somehow we can see that
the grasses are indeed native,
something in the way they

behave themselves
in the presence of company—
the child obedient,
speaking only when spoken to,

bluestem and grama and
purple lovegrass—
and standing beside my brother
I do it stoutly and for a

long time
into the Republican,
watching the cold clear water
carry it away, the ultimate

political ploy,
and thereafter we stand
quietly on the bridge,
all things under our eyes

distinct and clean,
and when I empty my pocket
we watch the coins settle
wavering and distant

among the small stones,
the face of a penny blurred
as the first step up from bondage
into a field of unaffected sunshine.

OTOE COUNTY IN NEBRASKA

On the run is the Otoe County corn rootworm,
overcome by laboratories:
who have purpled the soil with nuggets enough
to deter the deepest scavenger.
Thus as you drive the plush curvaceous trails
of Otoe County
you can sense the rootworm's grim retreat—
the dirty little no good
crop killing bugger
hightailing it for Kansas and Oklahoma,
for south Texas,
through Mexico
to a tip in Yucatan
from which it can throw itself
for mercy into the sea.
You can imagine it going without breakfast,
halfway now across the Caribbean,
dogpaddling its hundred thousand legs
to maintain a slim distance
between its life's little juice
and the laboratories that,
running at full throttle with periscope up,
cannot unlock their hatches until that
last little juice has been spilled.

Meanwhile, back in Otoe County,
the cornrows rise corpulent as green trees.
In a red Volkswagen you are a snail,
\ hunched and alien and terribly humble.

BLOOD

My hand is not the color of yours, but if I pierce it,
I shall feel pain . . . . The blood that will flow from
mine will be the same color as yours. I am a man.
The same God made us both.
    –Standing Bear

The nighthawk gyres on what we cannot see
but cannot live without.
Call this simple truth likewise
an acknowledgment of faith.

To put the test to what we know as fact
we'd hike to Shannon's pond where,
naked, we'd hold our breaths
to explore the wreckage

of a misbegotten Hudson, hold them
until our lungs were close
to bursting, then with a timing
always providential

we'd break the surface to inhale
no more deeply than
sweetly, my brother on one occasion
bleeding from an artery,

he having explored the Hudson
and its shards too closely,
and with a friend I helped
to carry him back to town, blood

between each twisting
of the tourniquet spurting
red and thick and communal, his
blood my blood, his blood the blood

of all of us yet breathing, all
thick and red, all brothers.

DROUGHT

Nobody wears clothes anymore,
not even the local virgin's
scarecrow.

The manikins in all the storefronts
have dropped their drawers
like so many hot potatoes.

One goat and three medium-sized children
have so far disappeared
down a split in the ground
behind the Champlin station.

Between two upright posts a length
of #9 wire whines like a Baptist's prayer
in a depraved wind.

Ham and eggs for half price, fresh
off the cement grill in front of Rocky's Café.

For one thin dime you can earn the privilege
of watching Roy Duncan start a fire
with his fingers.

Boll weevils gather like flies wherever
Vernon Ryan elects to spit.

Even the preacher's mistress has given
up the show, her high heels arrested in the pitch
of the pavement, her lipstick running like
chokecherry down the cleft of her chin.

It's no use: Hell has moved its headquarters
into southeastern Nebraska.

Far into the night the last of the dogs
keeps everyone in town awake
with its decision not to bark.

Boatmate

My boat is a green jonboat
christened *Our Lady of the Loup*
with a bottle of Lone Star Beer.

Loaded to the gills
it nonetheless draws no more
than five or six inches of the current
we drift in.

I sit at the oars
facing aft. So tell me, boatmate,
where we're headed. Then ask me, boatmate,
where we've been.

We take turns at the oars,
the one on relief reading the channel.
And when just now we find one, wide and deep,
I rest the oars, lean back,
ask my boatmate to fetch me a beer.

In four brief months his heart
will burst too suddenly, too
violently for anything
short of divine intervention
to save him. But today, this hour, this

moment he sits like an unlikely ornament
near the stern of *Our Lady*,
at his left the shoreline
replete with cattle and crops,
houses and trees and barns and beyond them
a blue-topped horizon
moving swiftly upstream,

and drunk am I before having finished
this first libation—not Lone Star, now,
but something else, something
filled with the ripeness of sun
and of motion, motion
uncanny with change into change,
yet empty of premonition.

That Voice From a Brain Evolved to Dream

for Loren Eiseley

We go into the hand-dug cave, my brother and I,
on our bellies down the slope of a tunnel
whose roof like the roof of the cave itself
sags with the criss-cross of pine and lath,
tarpaper and feedsack covered thickly with dirt
hauled up and out from the hole
where now with a match to the wick of a candle
we learn the meaning of secret, the truth of space.

The candle flickering
flickers my brother's face.
We have little to say:
the thrill of the cave has reduced us,
our open mouths the mouths of those first two carp
who amazed themselves by journeying just one step more
beyond that other step they took how many miles ago
away from water.

Damp the walls, after an early-morning rain
now seeping. Into a puddle my brother, barefoot,
works his toes. By the time the candle has spent itself,
my brother's feet, up to the ankles, up almost
to the high cuffs on his overalls,
are lost in ooze.

Earth, dark earth, is at the nose.
If we could see we might see
fingers scraping clay, inventing claws.
We speak, when at last we speak,
the croak of single syllables.

How long must we linger in this cave today,
my brother and I? Day into night,
night into long moist day, the thrill of the cave
reducing us on and on,
until the sound of a voice from a brain
evolved to dream
urges us to the flap at the top of the incline:

lord, you should see my little brother

with his snout
push through the flap,
should see him raising himself to his knees,
dirty little beautiful little lizard
stretching mightily to find its legs
in the Kansas sunshine.

We look around, oxygen tart as ginger on the tongue.
A hawk in the high blue sky is circling.
Except for the bird, we are alone—
that voice from a brain evolved to dream

                                          being

the warm soft indulgence of our own.

SAUNDERS COUNTY BARN

Try to ignore that Saunders County barn,
the one with the slatted, broken back,
where swallows in the dusk are homing.

Don't ask who the grandfather was
that called his milkcows to those brittle boards,
whether he had one offspring, or a dozen.

Don't concern yourself with the color of his teeth,
or inquire into the type of wood he fired
to burn the mortgage. Nor his wife:

whether she kept her wits past sixty,
or as a new bride drew blood when she
looked upon the back forty and bit her lip.

Nor their child, or children:
whether after one more final coat of paint
he/she/they hired an auctioneer. Or didn't,

and so hung on to be buried north of the toolshed.
Don't care whether the barn smells yet of dung,
whether the stanchions are yet slick

from the rubbings of cows' necks.
Don't bother even to ask after the swallows,
whether their droppings are mellowing in brittle hay.

Tell yourself that it has been a long and dusty day,
and that you must reach Wahoo by nightfall.
Thus, with firmness, tell the barn to go away.

Then glance at your rear-view mirror, where,
like a midget posing, relieving itself into the wind,
the barn grows smaller and smaller, then disappears.

Concentrate now on the road ahead.
Do not waste yourself on anything
lost, neglected, absent, weathered, or dead.

Bathing in the Loup

Buck naked and therefore vulnerable,
green jonboat tethered
to a cottonwood
thus far not molested by beaver,
I bathe myself until the fresh bar of Ivory

loses the letters of its identity.
If a goddess should happen along,
if I should look up to see her watching me,
would I be within my mortal rights
to strike her forever blind?

Sand no longer at home in the Sandhills
gives way beneath my feet. Sac and horn
float on the water as if bobber
and bait. I extend the lathering
to include the face, the hair. Eyes closed,

I give myself over to movement, this body
as if the unwieldy log that because
its resistance is low sooner or later will
get there. When eventually I rise, when
eventually my legs are steadied
against the current,

I will shake the river from my hair
to see already a half moon
skirting the clouds, and trusting its light
I'll return to the boat and the cottonwood,
to the spot where the goddess might have stood,

where I will build the fire.

Drifting

They that go down to the sea in ships, that do business in great waters; these see the works of the Lord, and his wonders in the deep. –Psalm 107:23-24

Going down to no great sea
To do no great business,
I lie relaxed on this
Moving water that knows
Its way even on windless

Days between pastured banks
And around fills of wispy
Shifting sand. The one-man
Rubber raft beneath me knows
No weight. It is seamed like peel

To the juice of my unmighty
River, and I to it. Face up,
Eyes closed, legs trailing
Like jointed driftwood,
I give myself to the river.

    The world is surplus,
    And only surplus matters.

The current tells me with
Its brief maelstroms that we
Are moving, while not even
A full sun can deny
Me darkness. I turn slowly,

Whorling from the sun, feeling
Change as the river changes,
We vulcanized to softness
Under undulations
Lighter than the lightness

Of cottonwood seed on water.
Peace is this, and the quick liquid note
Of a contiguous meadowlark,
The small sound hovering like flotsam
On the sun-washed crown of the river.

    Oceans fail.
    All ships of war have settled.

For less than sixteen dollars
I own what matters. Inflated
With my own breath, with air
That has touched all shores, my raft
Like forgiveness bears me up. We are

Breadless on no troubled waters,
Being blessed by the Navy's compassion
For leftovers that need
Somewhere to go, and someone
To go with, while waiting.

So in smallness we vagrants wait on,
In dizzying silence
Thankful for silence and smallness,
For the patient, diurnal sun,
For the current that flows in the river.

> *The USN is infinite*
> *In its concern for remnants.*

It is not my no great sea
That I am on, doing
No great business for no one
Great—except perhaps
A bit for the meadowlark,

Who perhaps accepts my sight
As I his sound. How could
He see me except that I
Be here? With long bare legs
I wash the water clean,

And with my outstretched hands
I give the river bones
To part its current with.
My hair stirs stillness
Into a slow cool breeze.

> *We live by drifting*
> *Only on borrowed things.*

Beside brush the current darkens.
Half asleep, I feel the shadows.
The wispy sand is high.
I shake myself into daylight,
And the bright world focuses.

My legs have turned the water
Shallow. The raft scrapes sand.
In drunkenness I stand
To find the lost current,
To portage over time

And over glistening grit
The confidence that though
Going down to no great sea
To do no great business
Is the business of no great king,

> *The world is surplus,*
> *And only surplus matters.*
> *Oceans fail.*
> *All ships of war have settled.*
> *The USN is infinite*
> *In its concern for remnants.*
> *We live by drifting*
> *Only on borrowed things.*

LOVE SONG AT MIDNIGHT

If there is magic on this planet,
it is contained in water.
            –Loren Eiseley, *The Immense Journey*

At midnight
I awaken to the sound

of moving water,
voodoo water, water

with its hocus-pocus never
ending, water that compels

whatever else is chiefly water
to acknowledge change that water

never ending must unendingly
promote,

I awake now in the silent tent
aware of change, this body

chiefly water changing,
voodoo body, body

with its hocus-pocus never
ending, body that arising

moves outside
beneath a yellow moon

to listen more distinctly
to water

moving, water
in me and beneath me

on this shoreline
changing, water

that will take me until it
having done so

further takes me.

MIRACLE ON THE WEST BANK OF THE RIVER

for John Walker

It begins with a guitar's
broken neck,

moves then to its unlikely
replacement,

an ancient Stella found
in a farm-

house attic by a farmer who
aware of our plight

delivers it into our hands,
two of which

with new strings, duct tape,
and immaculate

patience perform the delicate
and necessary

surgery until—behold!—Stella
clears her throat,

hums, begins to sing, her sound
concordant

with the sound the John Deere
made, Johnny

pop-pop-popper moving
heavily

from there to here to bring us
tidings of great

joy, for unto us a tune is born
again, the farmer

on his tractor
halfway across a continent

of stubble turning to wave,
good luck, boys,

good luck, you lovely numb-
nuts, in our hearts

meanwhile

something ringing—call it,
for want

of a better phrase, a melody
of love.

CORN

The corn cannot be patient forever.
If the clouds do not gather,
if the rain does not
reach down to the
raw and tender root,
the corn will die.
The stand that it takes in early summer
is mostly bluff,
a good green show for the customer.
But later, if the clouds do not send moisture
deep into the raw and tender
whiskers of the roots,
the corn will die.

The corn will die.
We repeat ourselves,
remembering all the time
that those we most admire
repeated themselves.
Under workshirts
our bellies heave inevitably with precedent.
Yes, surely, the corn will die.
Unless the clouds gather,
and the rain reaches down
to the raw and tender roots,
the corn will die.

The corn will die.
Saying it, we say, might help
to blunt that final barb
should the corn, in fact, die.
Because we are those
who cannot live by guile
or rich improvisation,
we must have our water

straight down from whatever it is
the dumb dependent call the heavens.
Or the corn will die.

And so it is that our necks stiffen,
our mouths suck at seaweed with the carp.

Beyond the window,
encircled by wire,
the corn, as if draining,
changes its color.
There are too many hours in the day,
and unless the clouds gather,
and the rain reaches down
to the raw and tender roots,
too many dog days in the year.

Riding My Bicycle Without Hands
Down Huntington Street

the secret children
has something to do with the circling
something to do with heft and with momentum
something to do with the urge
to look back over the right shoulder
only of ancient memory

which means that if virginia mae brown
could see me now she most certainly
would repent that most wretched
of all denunciations

don't look to walk me home
after choir wednesday nights
and don't come sniffing and ogling
into the kitchen for me
billy you creep for you
I have snapped my last bean

the poor child did not realize
the extent to which at forty-six
I should come to master this bicycle

I keep one eye on the front wheel
the other on a dumptruck
in my rear-view mirror
bearing down

with arms fully extended
I bless the grass the trees
the delicate bursts of flag and birdsong

I am giddy and far gone with the season
inebriate of place
of the breeze that makes a touchstone
of the eyes
the face

god is a handlebar in the sun
I give one hand to an old woman
dying on her front lawn
she accepts it kisses it revives
cackles hallelujah all the way to kingdom come

(what was it anyway I rode away
to be away from)

I give the other to the truck
which with a stub I christen the virgin brown
to its heft to its momentum
to spoke and wheel
like the color of midday in lincoln in nebraska
going around going down and around and around

SONG

I am haunted by waters.
　　—Norman Maclean, A River Runs Through It

When I need to walk,
I'll walk with the river.
When I need to talk,
I'll talk with the river.

The boy doesn't yet know it
but he will be haunted
for the rest of his life
by what he's in love with:
not largeness in the form
of Missouri or Mississippi,
but smallness in the form
of Niobrara, Elkhorn, Loup.

The yellow sand plum
is better off jelly.
The prickly pear
is best left alone.

Embarrassing, isn't it,
to be carrying a black lunch bucket
while others your age
are eating hot lunches, some
at school, others downtown. Even so,
the taste of sand-plum jelly,
at this time and later, as the taste
persists, makes embarrassment
worthwhile. And the bread,
so hot from the oven—the boy
can smell it late into
each afternoon.

The buffalograss
will make a fine cover.
The wild prairie rose
ain't seen, it's discovered.

When Sand Creek runs dry
the boy walks the lowest gully
where water should be. In bare feet

he discovers warmth
from the earth up. Looking at the sky,
blue and endless, he wonders
how much it will rain
when the next rain
comes around.

The cottonwood seed
so lightly dropping
delays its descent,
passing and stopping.

Some of the cottonwood branches
are brittle, some as dense, it seems,
and as unyielding, as rods
of steel. The boy,
about to strike a match to start a fire,
wonders why. And those bass
jumping now in the pond: when the boy
casts a jitterbug among them
why don't they bite?

When I need a friend
I can count on the river.
Drifting along,
Mother Nature delivers.

The spring house: each time
the boy goes there
there it is. So too the pond.
Each time, surprised, he
stands on the bank
for a long time,
taking everything in. And
though there is too much
ever to be taken in,
he takes it in.

Camping on the North Bank of the Platte

for Harvey Potthoff

Early evening,
and the young people are wading the river,
becoming bold in its clear shallow currents,
their laughter hanging distinct and immobile

in the warm and windless air.
They will not be surprised when later
the storm blows in, slapping the tents,
no more surprised when just as suddenly

the storm moves on,
when night with its myriad stars
settles over their luminous bodies
like a weightless comforter.

They are in love
with the inevitability of joy.
When they sleep
they sleep the insolent sleep

of the stone. O Lord,
how the power of the absence of guile
might buy and sell this world!
Mother, Grandfather, who was the first

to permit the dream its entrance
into the lizard's brain?
In our own sweet partial ways
we are immortal.

My Granddaughter, Almost 4, Throws 7 Small Stones Into the Platte River

That evening she wants to know
if they are still there,
if in the morning
we might be able
to find them.

We wade to each precise spot
where she knows she remembers
she threw them.

The water, I tell her,
has moved them downstream,
and she begins to walk
in the direction
I am pointing.
I follow.

She stops from time to time
to bend over
to bring up
to examine
a rock, a leaf, a twig,

until at last her fists are thick
with seven small stones.
We take them home and dry them off,
feed them, give them names,
show them to all our friends.

When they are fully grown
we carry them back
to the ongoing lotus of the river,
where one by one,
in mutual joy and pain,

we throw them in.

Part III
Stops Along the Way

"Listen to at least three languages:
the county's, the township's, the house."

–from Don Welch's
How to Live in Buffalo County

LATE EVENING ON THE NORTH BANK

I sit on the bleached-white trunk
of a cottonwood
watching the moon's reflection
in the Loup's slow-moving current.

First a guitar, then a banjo. Red-
haired Boy. Devil's Dream. I
take my turn at the amber bottle,
then pass it on.

Faces in something of a circle
flicker, washed earlier
by water, washed now
by flame.

On the surface of the moving water
a full milk moon, moon
of the shedding ponies,
seems not to move.

I pull an old Barlow from my pocket,
with its silver blade
begin the non-profit business
of essential whittling.

Darkness gathers itself into more
darkness. The whiskey
returns. Peaceful Easy Feeling.
Blackberry Blossom.

The campfire crackles
like an old man
who can't stop remembering
something funny.

In a Motel Room Somewhere
In Western Nebraska

Through the large window
I can see clearly too many stars
to be clearly taken in.
So many nights in this distant life
have I tried to sort out to understand
what can neither be sorted out
nor understood.

As a Tenderfoot, for example,
I lay on a pallet of blanket and bunchgrass,
studying the stars, the campfire
a torrid and fallen moon, the scoutmaster
in his puptent snoring. I fell asleep at last
empty-handed, in the outer space of mind
reached no conclusion.

Now, on the smaller window across the room,
Nolan Ryan with the Rangers
registers his seventh career no-hitter.
At 44 he is proof that hero is something more
than concept—he is the star with flesh on its bone,
though the nerve-ends in his arm remain
elusive as the wink in the eye of Venus.

Later, as an Eagle, I ascended no higher
than the ground I stood on.
Except to wonder, as tonight I wonder,
about the backdrop that makes the glory possible:
the darkness beyond the stars,
the batter in the bottom of the ninth,
two gone, the count at two and two,
going, as they say the earth and heavens go,
around, around.

OUTSTATE NEBRASKA, NOV. 21

The boys at the power plant are talking snow.

Outside of Thelma's Popper
the smell of buttered corn
balances on near icy air like some
firm unpainted farm girl
riding bareback.

In the pool hall hovered under smoke
quartets sit singing dominoes.

Beer lies in oak lakes at the bar.

Outside, Floyd Catlett sits a bench
that fifty years ago
might have been a mare.
He lips a fresh cigarette,
feeling his mackinaw for matches.

The custodian at the United Methodist Church
is wondering where to go
to ask a question or two
about thermostats.

The cook at Bake's Café expects a light supper run.

Judy Garland is at the Rialto.
Yellow bulbs blink on the marquee,
while low lamps light asphalt
up and down the street.

Breath goes neat as Sunday shirts.

From somewhere gloves clap.
Beyond the sound, darkness.
The heavy smell of clouds.

Snow, sure as hell!

Beside dynamos
the boys at the power plant
smile and spit stoutly
through their brown teeth.

This Tree, This Hackberry

This tree, this hackberry,
marks the center of the homestead well
the youngest of the Holcomb offspring
dallied into. The rescue effort failed.
Without a curbing, the walls,
as if on cue, had buckled in.
Just too much stress, they said,
against that vertical of mud and sand.

Fred the father planted the tree,
Joseph the middle son
the first of many to cut it down.
Behind a brace of mares
its branches made a vast ungainly harrow
to skim away the bunchgrass
on a long narrow strip
of new-cut ground.

Imagine the final step into darkness
deep as a mother's dream.
Imagine the roots of the hackberry,
loco for something damp and sweet,
reaching ten full fathoms downward,
there to discover a huddle of bone and marrow
that in another life had answered
to Rebecca Lynne.

Or would have answered,
had she not been so all-fired busy with the butterfly,
remarking the brilliance of the orange on its wing
under a high and mighty Cherry County, in Nebraska, sky.

THE MAD FARMER
SHUTS HIMSELF INSIDE HIS SILO
TO SING AWAY THE STORM

for and after Wendell Berry

Because the silo is round
each note is round,
each note eternity in a nutshell,
and knowing this the mad farmer
knows also that his song can never be lost,
that the notes will circle and circle
until the storm relents,
until the door left open permits them
freedom

and they will go then inevitable as seed
to the four corners of the universe,
there to put themselves together over and over,
becoming over and over the song
that now at the height of the storm
the mad farmer hat in his hand
stands singing:

O la and la and earth and water and wind,
sunlight and shadow,
la and la and hands deep into the soil,
and work and love,
and the greatest of these is work
and love and hands, la and la and
the immaculate equation of knowhow
and concern

until the silo spins with the mad farmer's song,
until the storm with its thunder and lightning
joins in,
la and la and crack and rumble,
and knowing these, and the fathers
and the mothers and the children of these,
the mad farmer hat yet dripping in his hand
invents a final verse, releasing each word
with its attendant note whole as faith
into the space that waits
to be more than itself
when the storm relents
and the sun does its own savage work
and the harvest behold! is in.

Saturday Special

In the Hunter's Lounge in Waco, Nebraska,
I watch a priest alone at a table
address the Saturday special:
smothered steak topped with mushroom gravy,
green beans, mashed potatoes, a generous
dollop of cole slaw.

He is the only one here with a tumbler of milk,
the only one here not talking with someone,
not laughing, not meeting someone's eyes,
not raising a schooner to propose a toast.

It isn't polite to stare, my wife says,
and of course she's correct. But it's difficult
not to watch him, difficult
not to make him the protagonist
in a screenplay worthy of Chekhov. Or
in a novel by Arnold Bennett, who,
having studied a pair of elderly women
dining near him in a small café,
hurried home and wrote *The Old Wives' Tale.*

With a few soft words my wife
returns me to our table. Pshaw, I say,
he doesn't know me from Adam's house cat.
That's not the point, she says, and of course
it isn't, the point being that I'm invading
someone else's solitude, solitude that
probably the priest enjoys, spirit enhanced
by the presence of flesh, my own flesh
in turn enhanced by the presence of spirit,
another libation tasting better, I'd swear
on a stack of Bibles, than the very first.

A Poem of Place

Ole's Big Game Lounge in Paxton, Nebraska,
is an anecdote listening at the keyhole
to catch the wind of its last line.

Say that it all began with the head of the antelope
that overlooks the shine on the bottoms
of Ole's chipped obedient beermugs:
how that very same set of antelope eyes
looked up one early morning
and straight into the blue dew-heavy barrel
of Ole's most recent, most uncontested rifle.
Say that Ole, whose fingertip had made, say,
most gentle love the night before,
squeezed the trigger into sweet, sulfuric flak,
into the instant snap and buckle of broken knees.

And say that it contained the leap of the cougar
at the soft distended neck of the doe,
both now arrested in pursuit and in flight
on a platform of unpainted pine
rigged by the purple thumbs of Ole's faithful
henchmen. To note the size and shape and sharpness
of the cougar's teeth,
read as if chiseled stone
the dark dilated pupils of the doe—
that dies, and lives, escaping,
while the cougar, sleek as a long-winded runner,
shall aways be about to do its share
of deadly cutting down and dying.

And say that on and on
and on and on it rambled:
scorn on the black, belated nose of the lesser kudu,
the shin of the gazelle so far, so fast from home
no sign, no map, no holy star avails.
A pheasant, on his last stilted legs,
is sorting out again the chiefest details:
the color of the morning, the texture of the soil,
the sharp, hopeless height of the stubble.
The polar bear, wide as a door,
rises rampant within a roped-off lawn—

beyond which reptilians whisper their innocuous venom
into the ears of the unfallen,
each an additional line:
wolverine and wildcat, badger and moose,
partridge and quail and caribou.
Beside a barrel of unmarked untapped beer
the thick mane of a North American bison
falls like an unfilled flag.

And say that once begun it must continue:
the next-door neighbor's Siamese
always about to flick its right front paw
into that softest spot on the snowbird's belly,
while Ole himself, greasing the gray of his apron
with the fat of his hands,
explains to a novice the difference between
the trap shooter and the skeet,
but all the time thinking how much better
that stranger at the end of the bar would look
if only his ears were curled to points,
if only his hide were tanned for moccasins,
if only his bloodshot eyes were blue,
and buttons.

Outside the Sheldon Gallery, Early June

In the sculpture garden a young dark woman
  in dark tights
    dances on and around a bronze reproduction

of Rodin's *The Thinker*,
  and when she assumes the young man's
    pose beside him

her form in the brilliant light of June
  is so constant I begin to wonder
    which form is which—

and maybe it's the heat
  or maybe the doctored cola
    I had for lunch,

but soon enough it's the bronze that's
  dancing,
    I swear it is,

The Thinker having had his fill of thinking,
  his body in liquid motion
    glinting golden in the sun,

the woman meanwhile
  deep inside the pleasured well of thinking,
    and when at last I move

I move as if related somehow both to
  river and to stone,
    my body watching my body turning

quickly ancient, my body
  watching my body static, but
    forever young.

Upon Winning First Prize
in the Hog-Calling
Contest at North Platte

Nebraskaland Days, June 18-25, 1978

I thank all of those hocks and chops
and snouts and loins
that made this moment possible.

If I had time,
and if the heat were something less than stifling,
I'd name them each and all.

Suffice it to say that I am elated
with the achievement, proud
of the father's father
who gave me the toenails and the torso
and the lungs to call such savory creatures
to the table.

Special thanks to the Salt Valley Pork Growers,
who encouraged me chiefly
by refusing to twist
my tail.

And thanks also to my manager, who helped me
through those awful days and months
and weeks and years
when I thought my spirit and my strength
must surely fail.

And, finally, thanks to all those shoats who stood
solid as polished glass before and beneath me
throughout the highest point
of this swift ordeal.

Nostrils flared, so lovely and so pink.

So vulnerable.

Moose Lodge, Saturday Night

Business at the punchboard is booming:
spend two bits, help a crippled child.

A woman with beersuds on her upper lip
is dipping her right arm
into the workings of her purse.
Already, she says, she has blown a small fortune.
If quarters alone can do it, she says,
you can look any day now for an end
to human suffering.

At the pool table a gentleman
with a pearl-handled cuestick
uncrosses his eyes just long enough
to scratch on the 8-ball.
He'll just have to settle, he says,
for another cold Blue Ribbon.

A sirloin for two sizzles and spits,
overlapping its platter.
On the dance floor
a lean girl in a seersucker blouse
is beginning to shimmy.

According to the loudspeaker,
Carl and Larena Ogden
have been married
precisely twenty-five years.

The last time I had kahlua and cream,
says the woman across from the sirloin,
I threw up my toenails.

And if that gal in the seersucker blouse
had something more than peanuts for mammaries,
she'd be slapping herself, and her partner with her,
clean into the middle of next Wednesday.

The Witching Hour

To me an ancient cottonwood is the greatest of trees
because in his youth he shaded the buffalo and wore
a halo of pigeons, and I like a young cottonwood
because he may some day become ancient.
  —Aldo Leopold, *A Sand County Almanac*

Yonder, legs hanging over the edge
of the riverbank, attaboy sculptor
sits with a length of cedar
carving another miniature
rendition of the human form.

It's the witching hour, everyone sated,
everyone doing what each one pleases.

I find a spot in the shade,
settle my back against a smooth
curvature of debarked cottonwood,
open my unabridged copy of *The*
History of Damn Near Everything.

I'd like to learn more
about the evolution of the zerk,
but it's the witching hour
and I'm not above being bewitched.
I think of Thucydides, or was it
Aristotle, who wrote that
happiness is what you find when
you're loafing up to your potential.

I therefore in pursuit of happiness
close first the book, next the eyes,
at which moment I learn again what
Longinus, or was it Paul the Apostle,
knew all along, that clean water, moving,
provides, for the common idler,
the natural world's most delicious sound.

I'm like this tree that is rooted
by the water: until
something more than what's happening
happens, I shall not be moved.

CORN-FED AND HAND-SPANKED

Remembering the Nebraska Cornhuskers
under Bob Devaney

It's what the man on television calls us
when our big-boned fullback
like a snub-nosed truck

flattens a host of would-be tacklers. Well,
golly dang and shucks, folks,
that's pretty much the way

we do things here in mid-America, hey-diddle-
diddle, right up the middle,
clean-cut and

smash-mouth and when it's over we grin
like gophers and wipe most
of the blood

from our noses before shaking hands. Meanwhile, stubble in the fields
lies waiting

to be turned under for the start of another far-off
season. Birds too many
to be counted

feed on the left-behind grain. Some of them,
the prettiest, a few of us
with itchy fingers

will bring down. You know what it smells like
to be in a corn-fed mother's
corn-fed kitchen?

To watch as she spanks a clump of dough
into a sweet corn-fed
submission?

Meanwhile, the voice on TV tells his listeners
how important it is
to *main-tain*

dis-ci-pline. *Yes-sireee Bob*, he says, his inflections
all cattywampus, *yes-
sireee Bob*, as

meanwhile a line of young women wearing not
much more than their skin
kick systematically

one imaginary ball after another high into the crisp,
well-washed endlessness of another
not quite yet depleted

afternoon.

Zoo Bar

Into the crowded bar a blind man
shuffles, his long white cane
witching for an ongoing absence
of impediments.

In his other hand
he balances a schooner
of beer, its foam the color
of his long and independent hair.

O the light of the world is Miller,
Old Style, Coors, Pabst,
Heineken, Budweiser.

Onstage: Baseline Johnny
and the Okie Dokie Blues Band.
The man at the electric guitar
wears a blue shirt with white script
that refuses to relent: Brooklyn Dodgers.

What the blind man cannot decipher
when he goes to the men's room: Kiss
my ass and call it love.

Baseline Johnny is a long time up
from Oklahoma
where his daddy lived a good life
preaching. O take me
back to Tulsa,
I'm too young to marry.

At a high oval table seven women
sit on high wooden stools
with their legs crossed
blowing ropes of smoke

in the general direction
of the stratosphere.

The blind man follows his cane
to the bar for another drink,
follows his cane then
back to an empty chair.

Earlier in the day a full June sun
reminded me of Mother: Don't
ever look at it for very long, son,
directly.

What do you suppose the blind man sees
on the screen of his everlasting
blackness? In deference
to yet another deception
I'll call it love.

In a Tent with My Brother on the North Bank of the Middle Loup River in Nebraska

Morning has broken, like the first morning,
blackbird has spoken, like the first bird.
    –Eleanor Farjeon

Suddenly it's breaking, morning, not falling apart but
coming together, light like the first light
filling the tent, twitterings

from the throats of the first birds causing my brother
to say that if only he had a weapon he'd
silence those twitterings

once and for all, they having awakened him pre-dawn
in the middle of a humdinger dream.
But I don't believe

him. He is all full of crap and joy, the latter no doubt
heightened by anticipation—because
if we can somehow manage

to pull on our socks and tie our bootstrings we will
soon be standing near a flame over which
bacon in a black iron skillet

will be sizzling, our colleagues nearby twittering and
stretching and snapping twigs to feed the
fire, colleagues who will tell us

they're both surprised and happy to see us resurrected,
cups of coffee they'll give us hot
as the first cups

to the touch, and the day will unscroll pretty much as
it did in the beginning, yet now and again
maybe different, sun yielding

to rain, say, rain to sleet into hail into an evening
whose calm will be made possible
by its preceding storm, stars

too many to make sense of reflected in the slowly
moving water all day we will have
moved on, my brother and I

meanwhile together in the tent pulling on our socks
and tying our bootlaces, tasks no more
challenging than tedious,

one of the Prime Mover's ways of making mortality
easier if not downright welcome,
my incorrigible brother

humming something I believe he is making up, his
imagination in high gear already, his
grin like the first grin

causing me to hurry, to tie the laces in knots so secure
you can bet your bottom dollar they'll
last, at the very least, forever.

At Howard's Pantry in Lincoln, Nebraska

for Jay Gerber

Because I am sitting
in the midst of wordsong and baconsmell
how can my cup not runneth over?

To keep it brimful the woman
whose face is mostly widesmile
tips a vessel, its contents hot and black
and everflowing.

I order what my colleague orders,
biscuits and gravy enough
to please if not overawe
the village mortician.

Through a window I can see that
in a farflung world
treelimbs are bending. Each time I inhale
I inhale deeply.

Thanks to Brother Parkinson
my colleague's right hand cannot stop
waving. Hello, whoever you are. Hello,
whoever.

His voice is soft and steady
and reassuring. No, life is not
yet a treadmill to oblivion. It is instead
biscuits and gravy and wordsong

and baconsmell, goodness and mercy
between us in the guise
of time neverending counting down.

Part IV
Name it Home,
and You Can Never Be Gone

"These Nebraska skies,
   they hold me like a mother,
   and bring a promise
   with their morning light.
   Like a song
   that is brother to your stories,
   they'll cradle you
   in your longest night."

–John Walker, *Nebraska Skies*

WHEREVER

But I am bound to this place,
wherever the dancing is done.
                    −Amy Fleury, "Wherever the Dancing Is Done"

Not only dancing
as in the ritual motions of ankle and thigh,
hip and wrist and elbow and spine,
all in a familiar syncopation, but also

in the shuffling and the plodding,
and in those pesky nettles
of indirection, wrong paths taken so frequently
we wouldn't quite know how to live

without them. On a day lacking
flute or cadence beyond the heartbeat
I wander the acreage as if it had just been
created—barbwire, bunchgrass, roadapple,

stone. I am alone on what in another age
was my grandparents' farm,
dancing, as my mother might put it,
like a toddler with two left feet—one step,

two steps, stumble,
fall—just beyond me the hill that these
two left feet must climb if they are to stand
where the eye might see more clearly

what nearness so clearly
obscures. O this is the dance that
defines itself by the nature of the earth
on which it deigns to be performed,

whatever the time or circumstance, wherever
the wind moves through the door
that opens when we think
of home.

Drifting the Loup

When the force that pulls us to the water
relents,
it becomes the force that, gathering,

calls us home. We meanwhile
narrow the eyes
to read the channel,

sand beneath us moving, but more
slowly,
cattle on either bank not seeming to care

that revelation for one is for the other
hearsay,
before us, in a wavering distance, a bluff

sufficient unto our deadest reckoning. True:
the yellow sand plum is better off
jelly. True:

the prickly pear is best left alone. We meanwhile
eventually would taste the jelly,
would meanwhile

eventually leave the prickly pear alone. When the oar
touches water it touches
what we came for,

something unashamedly and perpetually
moving, and moving with it
we become its movement,

that bluff ahead moving apparently
upstream to greet us,
to take us in,

at the final instant
to change its steady mind
like the steadiness we drove away from

to wave us on.

August 12, 1992

For having lived long enough
to know what's indeed enough, this
reward: a young bur oak,
rising now just west of Old Main,
those responsible standing in a circle
around it, I standing in the circle with them.

When the storm with its ice and snow blows in
this tree will bend but
not quite break, in time will right itself
to keep on growing.

And I think of the son in Sophocles' *Antigone*
as he tries to convince his father to relent,
to withdraw the edict that, if kept in force,
will destroy not only the son's beloved Antigone,
but likewise the son himself. Sometimes to bend,
he says, is to show mercy. Not to bend, sometimes,
he says, is to show an absence
of mercy, with misery an everlasting consequence.

We stand in a circle with the bur oak,
freshly planted, at its center. Today
I am old enough to know what's indeed
enough. This tree. This circle. This moment.

This family.

LET THEM

Let them go. Let them go traceless
through the high grass and into the willow-
blur, traceless across the lean blue glint
of the river . . . .
            —Angela Shaw, "Children in a Field"

And let them, when the time is right,
return. Let them reverse themselves

through the tall bluestem, their bodies
restored to what they were

before they disappeared so eagerly
into the overgrowth beyond the river.

At the table let them ask politely
for the bread their mothers

kneaded by way of love into, where-
upon let them eat until their bellies

stretch tight as drums with children
who'll one day wander traceless

into that land from which there's no
return—until, our lives in need of songs,

we let them.

AFTER BREAKFAST WITH MY WIFE
AT THE HY-VEE DINER

Softly on spring snow
I walk the twelve blocks
back to home,
an early-morning sun

about to burn its way
through a gray overhanging
of clouds. Where is the wind?
Where are the friends

who coughed their last
sweet bitter days
into a cauldron
sufficient beforehand to the brim?

Heavy with flakes
hang the limbs
of cedar and pine and linden,
cardinal on a green white bough.

This is the postcard
I would send. My wife
drove off to work,
where probably just now

she is speaking to youngsters
of their options,
preserving the baby
high among them. Meanwhile,

softly on spring snow
I walk the twelve blocks
back to home,
already on the lilacs

buds not far from bursting.
This is the postcard
I would send. Flake and cedar
and pine and linden,

cardinal on a green white bough.

CAR BODIES

Birds above,
a funeral below. Poetry.
    –Paul Eggers, *Saviors*

Along an extended stretch of lazy river
upturned car bodies form a last line
of resistance, metal bastion
intended to deflect the current to eat
away the shoreline of someone else's pasture.

On the hood of an old green Catalina
Chief Pontiac thrusts
his sleek silver head
with its sleek silver hair
upward into the eye of a clear morning's sun.

I squint to see if anything here
resembles the Bel-Air Chevy
my sweetie and I made love in,
one of our bare lustful feet
breaking the glass on the domelight.

In less than a moment it is evening,
rookie off on his own
after firewood,
veterans with martinis
talking supper. If we had a clear-channel

radio, and if the day were Valentine's, 1945,
we could tune in and listen—to the baritone
of Crosby singing *Don't fence me in*, maybe,
or reports of the firebombing, muted
but intense, of Dresden.

Feeding the Horses

for J. V. Brummels

It's a warm evening in July,
an evening without wind,
an evening when the smallest aroma
hangs like something tactile in the air,
so you can imagine maybe
how sweet, how stout the scent of horseflesh
as Jim with a bucket of oats
stands feeding the horses,
the sound of the oats from the bucket
to the base of the cut-down barrel
like the soft sudden splattering
of the rain we haven't had for untold ages,
though a gathering of clouds above the sunset
with its pastel edges
breeds a promise.

Jim with his empty bucket
leans into the choicest barb
on the barb-wire fence. Someone,
no name specified,
left a gate open day before yesterday
and a fair-sized heifer worth her weight
in more than local currency
found liberty a temptation too aromatic
to resist, and if I don't find that
little sweetheart soon, Jim says,
my entire beleagured family
might kiss this lovely planet adios
hungry.

The horses meanwhile stand
nuzzling oats,
the haunches of their horseflesh
quivering. A flat slab of lightning
defines the edges of the gathering clouds.
Because the evening has no wind

the scent of flank and of rump and of fetlock
gently overwhelms. I think of the lost heifer
trembling in the sweet, sweet clover
of her freedom. The horses meanwhile
with their long indulgent faces
inhale the base of the cut-down barrel
clean. They are Blue, the smallest,
and Jody, the mother,
and her son with those circles of brown
on the mass of its luminous body
secure at home,
Cheyenne.

My Old Friend the Artist

for Reinhold Marxhausen

My old friend the artist
   guides me through a
      marvelous muddle

of tile and of stone, of iron
   and copper and shingle
      to the far end of his workshop,

where he shows me a large oil painting
   of a young woman
      standing

beside a young man sitting
   straight as a length
      of lumber

on a piano stool. *This is where*
   I came from, my old friend
      says,

his right arm sweeping the canvas,
   and this, he says,
      leading me again

across a vast complexity of rod and
   of rim, of fabric
      and clay, *this*

is where I am going. He points
   to a pine coffin with its lid
      at a high angle

open, and I can detect somehow the artist's
   infallible expertise,
      angle and bevel

and no discernible seam, my old friend
   meanwhile fitting himself
      prone as anything flat

you might imagine into the coffin, his grin,
    when at last he releases
        the pose,

a surprising extrapolation from the mouth
    on the young man in the
        painting, his eyes

when he opens them the damp limpid blue
    of his mother's. *But*
        just now,

my old friend the artist says, rising
    as if Boris Karloff
        from the bottom

of a mystery that has no bottom, *just now*
    I am somewhere in between,
        and more quickly

almost than possible he is out of the coffin,
    standing then waist-deep
        in a clutter

of raw essentials, reaching for something
    already created that
        he might use

for his own creation—God with dust in one
    hand, lines that just seem
        to go on and on

in the palm of the diminishing other.

Heart Attack

for Don Welch

Don, what I know about pigeons
you could extract from a silk hankie
and not be a magician. Pigeon-*hole,* maybe,
because God knows I have shelved
much of the puzzle of my life
without bothering to return
to reassess the pieces.

And likewise pigeon-*toed,* and certainly
pigeon-*livered.* But your homers,
that elite corps of beak and of plumage
you love, I believe, in ways
we birdless dolts can never understand—
they must surely be an extension of yourself,
you the bird who in spite of hell and high head-winds
returns, your flight steady, direct, strong,
the feral in you having been humbled
by the potency of home.

You write that you are back in the nest now
with an expensive piece of metal
positioned just so
to keep a coronary artery open. Christ! Let it
do its work. And let your own work
thrive and molt with the seasons,
each word a pinion the lack of which
so many of us otherwise hearty creatures
must surely die from.

Pioneer Burial

The soot that had been rubbed like lotion
Into the soft pine of the young lady's coffin
Stains the palms of the pallbearers,

Who after the lowering and the covering
Wash themselves with the cemetery's
Tall green prairie grass,

The sound of the sawing of their hands
Making it clear how little they approve
Death's lingering.

WINDSONG

to the memory of Paul Leibman

That late afternoon in early autumn, returning home,
my friend and I roll down the windows
to let the windsong in. *O it's a long, long way*

to Tipperary, it's a long way to home. Not Tipperary,
of course, but Broken Bow. And Ogallala.
And Anselmo and the swatch of prairie where we sit

beside a campfire, windsong having changed its tune:
Now the day is over, night is drawing
nigh. Shadows of the evening steal across the sky.

The truth is this: Neither of us owns the red pickup
that brought us here, it having been
borrowed from a neighbor who bought it new

as a last-moment gift to himself, an indulgence that
in spite of his Puritanic frugality
he could not resist, his melanotic cancer being well

on its way to a pyrrhic victory. Take it, he told us,
his voice a whisper, an almost silent
windsong. Here are the keys. Take them and take

it. So we took it. Not to Tipperary, but to Hyannis.
And Paxton. And Hay Springs and
the swatch of prairie where now beside a campfire

we clink our schooners to toast first the campfire,
next the neighbor and his new
red pickup, then last our journey, windsong

now a crooning through the nearby cornstalks—
and later, the campfire no more
than a soft depletion of coals, there is nothing

but the windsong of our breaths inside the tent,
this night, as always,
turning, as the worm turns, toward the morning.

CABOOSE

for Ray Judds

On a hill overlooking the Platte
a Burlington caboose
blooms greener than the grass
it rises from,
spoiling, no doubt,
the dream of that demented switchman
who one day sent it screaming
headlong with the grasshoppers
to this high wide pale
of vast inertia.

Aunt Vera I think it was
who said she saw the end of something
once just south of Kiowa or
was it Tulsa?
But pressed for details
she slacked her jaw,
picked at her lower lip,
conceded at last to silence.

Death. Kiss it off.
Have it straight from the conductor's own
calciferous mouth.

There is no such animal.

LAKE McCONAUGHY, MID-JULY

Green leaf from a growth I cannot name
sweetens the tongue. I chew. I salivate.
I become the bovine standing wide and solid
in the pasture. Ruminant. Cud. Drool. Slobber.
O where is the boy I trust to find me,
to nudge me with his simple stick,
to lead me home?

*

Here in this verdant hollow
an absence of sound confronts the ear:
no bickering, no clash, no clamor, no
one voice raised against another.

*

I stand swaying with the swaying of the trees,
body now unsteady, body warm, inebriate,
body now irregular in its rhythms.

*

Because the wind arranges and rearranges
the leaves on the cottonwood,
shadows fall silent. O
have you heard the latest rumor?
Never again will this old earth
be sanctified by water.

*

I am therefore myself the boy I trust
to find me, to nudge me with his simple stick,
to lead me home: no bickering, no
clash, no clamor, no one voice raised
against another.

No Longer Believing in Wind

for Jack Ernst

From the airborne dust we learn alliances:
at the most unlikely moments
we too settle among the veins of old leaves,
cozy into the corners of unsung barns.
Less solvent than snow,
we fill the hollows of our forebears,
those slow rocks of the fields.

Our flights are fancies
no more enduring than the movements
of small wings.
Always there is the pull
of something deeper than our thrust,
of something loftier even
than our wild propulsions.

And so it is we find ourselves
reduced to birth:
brother to brother descended,
in league with the center of the earth.

On the Oregon Trail
in Western Nebraska

Because the busted pod of the soapweed smells like home
I go a final time to pillage my grandmother's garden.
There I am, standing knee-deep in tomatoes
and onions and peavines, there I am bending over

to disengage the shell I'll split from stem to stern
to tongue the seeds, to inhale the hulls of the boats
they came from, and probably I shouldn't be doing this,
probably my grandmother wants and needs the fruits

of her German labor, but lust, they say, never knew guilt
or conscience, so there I am, transgressor kneeling
in the midst of my grandmother's plenty, fists adrool
with onion and pea and tomato, and if you look closely

you'll see my grandmother, there she is, standing
barefooted on the unpainted pine of the porch,
her short thick arms as if tentacles embracing her breasts,
and though I am much too involved to see her I know

her, know how uncommonly proud she is of her grandson,
how when she suddenly shouts she'll be calling no more
to him than to all those others from the old country,
brothers and uncles, fathers and mothers and aunts, and if you

look again closely you'll see both him and his grandmother,
there they are, the thief and the prodigal, both grinning, a
crack through the center of the sepia snapshot
unable to disjoin the blood in their mutual hands.

IN A PUMPKIN PATCH NEAR ROCA, NEBRASKA, EARLY EVENING

Ah the moon
having gone forth
has multiplied,
its orange offspring
lying everywhere

swaddled in the scent
of spilled October seed.
And I'm here
like your pet bovine
with a bell on—here

to find me the perfect
pumpkin. So listen:
anyone not gone
giddy with love
must leave the premises

tout de suite. I'll meanwhile
wander this field of plenty
until I can endure it
no longer,
until the last of the flat-

bed wagons circles
home—home, where summer's
purple grapes have
simmered themselves
into jars of jelly

translucent with desire.
Ah get up there,
full harvest moon,
rise high, sweet daddy,
climb that dark ladder

like the boy on his way
to the aromatic barnloft
one more time.

LANDSCAPE

We are the children of our landscape; it dictates
behavior and even thought in the measure to which
we are responsive to it.
       —Lawrence Durrell, *Justine*

To be *of* the landscape is not to possess it,
but to be part of it, an extension,
an offspring.

To honor the landscape is to borrow from it
a measure of its inexorable
beauty—limb

and leaf, feather and hide, root and bark and
blossom—wearing and breathing
and absorbing them

as acknowledgments of both necessity and
celebration. To be *of* the landscape is not

to defy it, but to take it in, to say what it says
when we come to its door,
You are welcome.

CRAZY HORSE: FINAL REFLECTION

The heart of Crazy Horse
lies throbbing in a box
that was not long enough.

So they cut him in half,
and on a pony drag delivered him
to somewhere just this side of Pepper Creek.

No one knows the precise spot,
they say. They say,
wherever it is,

that place must now be covered
high with prairie brome
whose roots reach down,

they say,
to catch the throbbing
of the heart of Crazy Horse,

to send the drumtap
up and out and over
all the earth:

It does not matter where this body lies,
for it is grass,
but where this spirit is, there
it will be good for all of us to be.

IN THE DISTANCE

In the distance the silo is too small
to hold the corn those endless fields
promise to yield.

Cross my heart and hope
to die. Stick a needle
in my eye. But

in the distance the Devil is busy
assuming the shape of a massive low-
slung cloud that

we'll remember as the reason the silo
became the echo chamber youngsters
from a nearby town

repeated themselves in. Now the silence.
The lingering scent of grain.
And looking up,

you can see an unbroken circle in which
distance, without boundaries,
is contained.

INSTRUMENTAL

At the moment it's All in G
on the banjo, notes
precise, cat-quick and clean
sent out and up
to whatever has ears to listen.

Without words the message
makes consummate sense,
without words no tower
with its forked, dissenting
tongues babbling.

Maybe this is pretty much
the way it was meant to be,
if anything is,
melody the sole arbiter
leveling pride and prejudice,

spite and greed, deceit and
inhibition. O brothers and sisters!
In the beginning was the word
restrained, its deadly decipherings
on hold until the music stops

and the word like the snake it
so often is
returns.

OF HAIR AND THE COMBING OF HAIR

Bending, I bow my head
And lay my hand upon
Her hair, combing, and think
How women do this for
Each other.
       –Gladys Cardiff, "Combing"

Here is the story my late friend Mary
told me,

story of hair and of the combing of hair,
how her

mother's last request was this: Would
you comb

my hair? And she combed it, Mary said,
combed

its whiteness into a compliance so soft to
the touch

that she touched it again and again. And
her mother

with her bird-frail fingers reached to
touch it

also, and at the touch her mother
smiled, she

said, and that was it—hair and the combing
of hair, and

the touching of hair with the tips of one's
fingers. And

that was the story my late friend Mary
told me.

Mowing the Lawn for the Last Time

I do it shortly after sunrise,
after the first hard freeze,
each swath a shredding
of leaf and of blade and of frost,
each swath so green, so perfect
I pause time and again to look
down the row to inhale as well as
to see it, to take it all in.

And the sound of the mower: a red
Piper Cub against a blue sky,
circling. Which is why
I do not hear my wife
at first when she calls me.

We sit on elm stumps drinking black coffee
from thick white porcelain cups
left from the days of her dead father's
café. I remember the waitress
whose face, it was said, could sour
milk, how the regular customers
loved her. We hold the cups
with both hands, leaning our faces
into them. The morning
for a few moments with us
stands still. We are very happy.

Nebraska: This Place, These People

All across the sandhills
and down the panhandle
and back across again
and up the Missouri into Omaha,
this place, these people,
blaze like firebushes.

An old woman in Wahoo punches her thumb
into the soil,
and fourteen babies in Weeping Water
give thanks.

Atop the capitol at Lincoln
a statue with a satchel at his side
is always about to scatter
the promise of next year's breakfast.

A young lover not far from Thedford
spitshines the manure
on his best boots.

Valentine opens itself to sunshine
hot as a kiss.

Catfish and carp are warming themselves
like beach bums
in the shallows of the
Platte and the Elkhorn and the Loup.
From the south-southwest a breeze
trembles cottonwood seed
like friendly flak
toward a Dakota border.

A covey of quail
struts the main street of Brownville
like vaudeville troupers up from the dead,
claiming first privilege.

On the outskirts of Macy Reservation,
in the weeds by the highway,
an ancient Indian and a shag buffalo

whisper to each other
through the thin skin
of an outnumbered nickel.

Nebraska.
This place, these people
blaze like firebushes.

Water and soil and wind,
color and light and heat:

something forever plump and firm
above the ground,
the urge forever
of something small but ripening

underneath.

SONG

These Nebraska skies,
they hold me like a mother,
and bring a promise
with their morning light.

> When the boy opens his eyes
> he sees nothing but sky,
> the color blue lightened
> and intensified
> by a high August sun.

> He turns his head to see
> his father standing
> tall beside and above him,
> father in blue overalls
> soaked dark with pondwater.

Like a song
that is brother to your stories,
they'll cradle you
in your longest night.

> The boy moves his head
> to see again the sky.
> It is the water
> inverted
> he'll dream of when
> this present dream ends.

So hold me here
when I have fear of dying,
of changing things
in some unknown tomorrow.

> The boy is not dead
> because his father
> in blue overalls

> pulled him
> from the water,
> with two fingers

missing from one hand
pulled him
from the spring-fed

pond. To be alive
is to be free
of the water your

lungs went swimming
in. And the father:
he seems taller now,

though even so
not very tall,
than he has ever been.

Hold me where
Nebraska skies around me
will tell my soul
your story's never done.

Now when the boy lies
on his belly
in the spring house
he drinks not only
water but also
the life of the unborn
fish. He rises
to stand watching
cold water rise
to flow out of its
trough and out
of the spring house
to lose itself
in a clean and
relentless stream.

And so it goes:
our story's never done.

ACKNOWLEDGEMENTS

The title poem, *Nebraska: This Place, These People,* was first published in **Prairie Schooner,** copyright University of Nebraska Press, Fall 1976.—The last stanza of *Crazy Horse: Final Reflection,* slightly revised, is from John G. Neihardt's **Black Elk Speaks.** The italicized sections in the first *Song* are from **Loup,** written by John Kloefkorn; the italicized sections in the second *Song* are from **Nebraska Skies,** by John Walker. Most of the poems in this collection first appeared in some of my earlier books. Thanks to the editors and publishers of the following:

Among the Living (Sandhills Press, Main-Travelled Roads #17, 1999): *Lake McConaughy, Mid-July* (reprinted in **In a House Made of Time,** Logan House Press, 2010).

Burning the Hymnal (A Slow Tempo Press, 1994): *Frank Fairchild: Young and a Bachelor and a Farmer.*

Collecting for the Wichita Beacon (Platte Valley Press, 1984): *Waiting for the Bus at 63rd and Huntington.*

Cottonwood County (with Ted Kooser, Windflower Press, 1979): *Riding My Bicycle Without Hands Down Huntington Street; Lake Leba, Early Spring; December Storm; Upon Winning First Prize in the Hog-Calling Contest at North Platte; Crazy Horse: Final Reflection.*

Covenants (with David Lee, Spoon River Poetry Press, 1996): *Bur Oak.*

Dragging Sand Creek for Minnows (Spoon River Poetry Press, 1992): *In a Pumpkin Patch Near Roca, Nebraska, Early Evening; Feeding the Horses; Outside the Sheldon Gallery, Early June; In a Motel Room Somewhere in Western Nebraska.*

Drinking the Tin Cup Dry (White Pine Press, 1989): *The Mad Farmer Shuts Himself Inside His Silo to Sing Away the Storm* (reprinted in **The Mad Farmer Poems,** poems by Wendell Berry, Press on Scroll Road, 2008); *Pissing into the Republican.*

Fielding Imaginary Grounders (Spoon River Poetry Press, 2004): *My Old Friend the Artist; Surprise Lilies; Zoo Bar.*

Going Out, Coming Back (White Pine Press, 1993): *Schwinn.*

Houses and Beyond (Platte Valley Press, 1982): *That Voice from a Brain Evolved to Dream; Behind the Movie House, Early July.*

In a House Made of Time (with David Lee, Logan House Press, 2010): *Mosaics; Saturday Special; Heart Attack.*

Let the Dance Begin (State Street Press, 1981): *This Tree, This Hackberry; My Granddaughter, Almost 4, Throws 7 Small Stones into the Platte River* (reprinted in **Platte Valley Homestead).**

A Life Like Mine (Platte Valley Press, 1984): *Mowing the Lawn for the Last Time.*

Loup River Psalter (Spoon River Poetry Press, 2001): *Late Evening on the North Bank; Love Song at Midnight; Boatmate; Song* ("When I need to walk..."); *Happy Hour; Song* ("These Nebraska skies..."); *Car Bodies; Bathing in the Loup; Instrumental.*

Not Such a Bad Place to Be (Copper Canyon Press, 1980): *Pioneer Courtship* (reprinted in **Treehouse: New & Selected Poems,** White Pine Press, 1996); *Corn* (first printed in **Voyages to the Inland Sea** (with Hale Chatfield, Center for Contemporary Poetry, Murphy Library, University of Wisconsin-La Crosse, 1977); *Moose Lodge, Saturday Night; A Poem of Place; Middle Loup; Drought; No Longer Believing in Wind; Pioneer Burial; Wet Spell; Nebraska: This Place, These People* (reprinted in **Treehouse: New & Selected Poems,** White Pine Press, 1996); *Caboose; Reflection; Drifting* (reprinted in **Treehouse: New & Selected Poems,** White Pine Press, 1996).

Out of Attica (Backwaters Press, 2008): *Miracle on the West Bank of the River.*

Paddlefish: *Corn-Fed and Hand-Spanked.*

Platte Valley Homestead (Platte Valley Press, 1985): *Platte Valley Windmill; Boundaries.*

Still Life Moving (with Carlos Frey, Wayne State College Press, 2006): *Blood; Of Hair and the Combing of Hair; Landscape; Tremolo; Let Them; River; Wherever; Miracle; What the Sky Says; What the Land Says* (the last two poems first appeared in the *Omaha World-Herald).*

Sunrise, Dayglow, Sunset, Moon (Talking River Publications, Lewis & Clark State College, 2004): *Drifting the Loup.*

Uncertain the Final Run to Winter (Windflower Press, 1974): *Otoe County in Nebraska; Some Directions for the Touring of Westcentral Nebraska; Outstate Nebraska; The Exquisite Beauty of Southeastern Nebraska; Cottonwood; Midlands Profile; Saunders County Barn* (reprinted in **Treehouse: New & Selected Poems,** White Pine Press, 1996).

Walking the Campus (Lone Willow Press, 2004): *Walking the Campus; August 12, 1992; After the Ice Storm.*

Wellsprings: Poems by Six Nebraska Poets (University of Nebraska at Kearney, 1995): *On the Oregon Trail in Western Nebraska* (reprinted in **Covenants,** with David Lee, Spoon River Poetry Press, 1996).

Where the Visible Sun Is (Spoon River Poetry Press, 1989): *Camping on the North Bank of the Platte; Nebraska, Early March* (reprinted in **Treehouse: New & Selected Poems,** White Pine Press, 1996); *Alone in the Sandhills of Sheridan County, Nebraska, Standing Near the Grave of Mari Sandoz* (reprinted in **Treehouse: New & Selected Poems,** White Pine Press, 1996); *After Breakfast with My Wife at the Hy-Vee Diner.*